200

VICTORIAN NOSEGAYS

Text by Pamela Westland
Illustrations by Gill Tomblin

CRESCENT BOOKS

Editorial Direction: Joanna Lorenz
Art Direction: Bobbie Colgate-Stone
Production Control: Susan Brown
Hand Lettering: Leonard Currie

First published in 1991 by Pyramid Books,
an imprint of Reed International Books, Michelin House,
81 Fulham Road, London SW3 6RB.

This 1991 edition published by Crescent Books,
distributed by Outlet Book Company, Inc.,
a Random House Company,
225 Park Avenue South, New York,
New York 10003

Printed and bound in Spain

ISBN 0-517-05260-1

87654321

CONTENTS

$\mathscr{I}$NTRODUCTION

THE VICTORIAN LOVE of flowers and plants found its
prettiest expression in the posy, or nosegay. Elegant
journals of the day showed designs and colour schemes of
posies to suit all manner of special occasions, and it was
the custom for ladies to take one to their hostess when
they went out to tea. The most popular design, now
considered a classic of the late nineteenth century, was a
round posy composed of concentric rings of flowers and
leaves arranged around a central flower, usually a rosebud.

4

The Victorians adored roses, and they loved deep and vibrant colours, so all the shades of maroon, magenta, crimson, scarlet, and deep blush pink of old-fashioned roses were perfectly suited to posy designs. Deep dusky blue, another favourite, was added in the form of hyacinths, grape hyacinths, and bluebells.

Flowers for posies were often cut from their stems and mounted on wires. This was done so that the false stems could be bent and shaped at will, and to make the "handle" more slender and elegant to hold. Glass of all kinds, coloured, cut crystal, pressed, moulded, or painted, was popular for containers, and there were even special posy holders, metal tripods supporting a bowl, which raised the posy high above the tea-things.

Not all Victorian posies were wired or even tied. A favourite table decoration was a flat posy of foliage and perhaps some flowers, arranged on a plate or at the foot of an epergne, a pedestal stand.

The Victorian period was the time when the language of flowers was at its height. Shy young men gave their sweethearts posies in which each component had a symbolic meaning of love, affection, sincerity, regret, or longing. If a maiden touched a flower to her lips, the answer was "yes". If she let a petal fall to the ground, her reply was "no".

Posies for a bride and her bridesmaids to carry; one to present to a special guest or to say "thank you" to a friend; a posy created for your own enjoyment – whatever the reason or the occasion, you want every posy you make to look its enchanting best for as long as possible. That means choosing or cutting flowers that are not yet fully open, recutting the stems slantwise – cutting them actually under water helps too – and giving them a good long drink of water in a cool place, overnight if possible. You will find a bunch of thin and medium gauge florist's wire helpful to mount small cones and nuts, to separate florets such as stephanotis and hyacinth, and to mount flowers with heavy or woody stems such as roses. Bind the false wire stems with gutta percha or green gummed tape to give them a more natural look and feel, and, especially if a posy is to be carried or presented, make sure that the "handle" – the bunch of stems – is as neat as possible. Whenever posies are to be without water for any length of time, spray them all over with a fine mist of cool water – do this over and over again in hot weather – and keep them in a cool place, even in the refrigerator.

When posy flowers and foliage are left on their natural stems, treat them as any other vase flowers, and place them in the prettiest container you can find. Victorian scent bottles, cosmetic jars, wine glasses and carafes, decorative bowls, a pretty cup and saucer, or a dainty teapot all make attractive containers. And on a special day, if the sun is shining, wear a posy on your dress, pinned to a belt or purse, or in your hat.

HEART-SHAPED VALENTINE POSY

Select about 14 partly-opened red rosebuds, a cream rose, a handful of snow-white gypsophila, and some frondy leaves like fern or carrot. Cut off the rose stems and twist the flowers onto medium-thick wires. Hold the cream rose in your hand and surround it with gypsophila. Arrange the rosebuds, bending the wires to coax them into a heart shape. Surround the posy with more gypsophila and a collar of leaves. Bind the stems together with wire and then with cream satin ribbon.

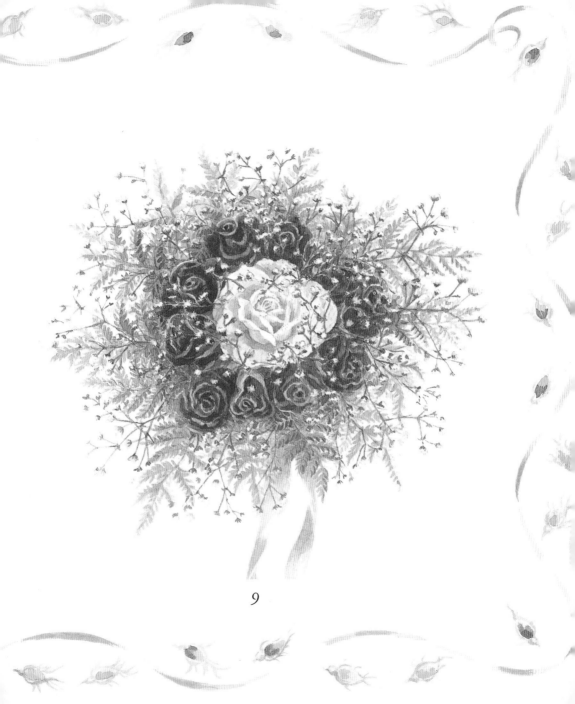

PRIMROSE & VIOLET POSY BASKET

*Pick a handful of violet and primrose flowers with
their leaves. Arrange about 20 violets in a cluster,
surround them with leaves, and tie the stems with
raffia. Make tiny posies of primroses in the same
way, using about 10 flowers in each. Arrange the
posies in a shallow dish in a pretty basket, or place
them in a cluster of tiny glasses or spice jars. On a
special day, wear a tiny posy on your hat.*

10

11

COUNTRY WEDDING MARIGOLDS

Gather a handful of Queen Anne's lace (or wild carrot) from the wayside, a bunch of yellow and orange garden marigolds, and a few cream-coloured spray carnations. Arrange the marigolds and carnations to make an informal bunch, then press stems of Queen Anne's lace between the flowers to cover them like a bridal veil. Bind the stems and push them through a hole in the centre of a double circle of white net. Tie with a narrow netting bow.

13

SCENTED LAVENDER & OLD LACE

*Gather a handful of sweet-scented lavender flowers,
and tie them into a tightly-packed bunch.
Surround them with pretty lime green stems of
lady's mantle (it's also called alchemilla mollis)
and then with a few wispy dried oats. Bind the
stems together with raffia, and tie them with a bow
of narrow ribbon lace in deepest cream. Display
the posy in a pretty cosmetic bottle on the dressing
table or in a linen-and-lace drawstring bag
on the bedpost.*

14

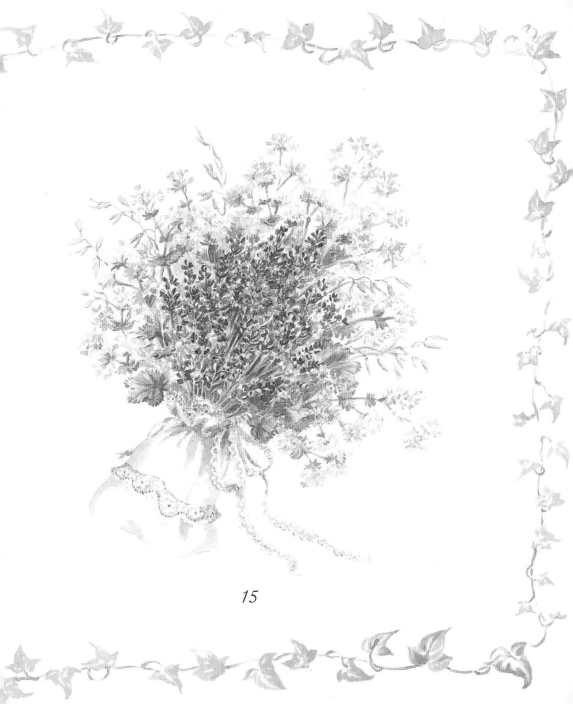

15

VICTORIAN ROSEBUD POSY

*Take some tightly curled rosebuds in deep and
palest pink, some double white pom-pom daisies,
and a pink and green hydrangea flower, after it's
had a long drink of water. Twist each group of
hydrangea florets onto a thick wire. Placing a
rosebud in the centre, arrange the flowers and
florets in rings, alternating the colours. Edge the
posy with ivy leaves. Bind the stems with pink
ribbon, and tie on a bow of crisp pink netting.
Pretty for a young bridesmaid or flower
girl to carry!*

16

17

Early Spring
Bridal Posy

*Take a bunch of fragrant paper-white narcissi, a
single stem of blue hyacinth, some yellow freesia,
and some silver-grey leaves – ballota, for example,
or sage. Pick off each flower and floret, and twist
thin wire around the calyx or base to make a false
stem. With a narcissus in the centre, arrange the
flowers in rings, the hyacinth florets separating the
pale colours. Arrange the leaves around the
outside, and bind the stems with wire. Wrap yellow
satin ribbon around the "handle" and finish
with a bow.*

19

DAINTY BRIDESMAID'S POSY

For a little bridesmaid or flower girl: take a handful of primroses and violets with their leaves and divide them into tiny bunches surrounded by foliage. Also take some grape hyacinths and 7 or 8 peach-coloured roses. Hold a rose in your hand and arrange the violets and primroses in circles around it. Alternate groups of 2 or 3 grape hyacinths with roses around the outside, and bind the stems. Push the posy through a hole in the centre of a paper doily, and secure it with sticky or Scotch tape. Wrap the stems with ribbon.

VICTORIAN-STYLE DOME OF SWEET PEAS

*Mixed colours of sweet peas shaped into a generous
dome make an unusual wedding posy. Take a
bunch of sweet peas in pink and purple, maroon
and mauve, red and royal blue, and cut the stems
in graduating lengths. Compose them in your hand
to form a ball shape, cut the stems level, and bind
them with raffia. Tie narrow baby ribbons in sweet
pea colours into multiple bows with
long trailing ends.*

23

BRIDAL BASKET
OF GARDEN FLOWERS

Find a shallow basket with a tall horseshoe-shaped handle, and line it with crisp white paper doilies, pressing the scalloped edges over the rim. Make small posies – about 6 to 7 – of pink, blue and white cornflowers and long-stemmed lawn daisies, with about 10 or 12 flowers in each. Arrange them standing up so that they are packed tight in the basket. Wire one posy low down on one side of the handle and tie it with narrow trailing ribbons.

25

SWEET-SMELLING GARDEN CLUSTER

*Collect together the sweetest-smelling flowers you
can find – rosy-pink, purple and white garden
pinks, which used to be called gillyflowers in
Victorian times; mauve, pink, and white freesias;
and rosy-pink honeysuckle. Make a dome of the
round, frilly-edged pinks. Surround it with the
trumpet shapes of the freesias and then with the
wild-looking spiky honeysuckle flowers. Tie the
bunch with several strands of raffia and finish with
a bow. Display it in a pretty vase in a bedroom.*

27

Aromatic Herb Tussie-Mussies

Even before Victorian times, people used to make
scented posies from herb leaves and flowers, called
tussie-mussies, and carry them from room to room.
Gather a mixed bunch of herbs — there could be
golden marjoram, pineapple mint, purple sage,
silver curry plant or lavender leaves, glossy bay
leaves, and creamy-white feverfew flowers (also
known as pyrethrum parthenium or bachelor's
buttons) — and tie them into small posies with a
"ribbon" of long chives. You might like to place
them in pretty wine glasses on the dining table.

29

VICTORIAN

FLOWER MESSAGE

By choosing the ingredients according to the Victorian language of flowers, you can compose a token that is full of hidden meaning. Choose, for example, a centifolia, or cabbage rose, to be a "messenger of love", red double pinks to signify "pure undying love", and ranunculus to say "you are very attractive". Surround the posy flowers with fern leaves for "sincerity", and trails of ivy for "friendship and marriage". To be sure your message gets across, you could enclose a card detailing each individual meaning!

31

A Gift From a Country Garden

Pick a bunch of garden flowers – there could be roses, pinks, sweet peas, scabious, and lady's mantle – and some long leaves, Solomon's seal or hosta for example. Place the leaves on a table top, arranged in a fan shape. Cover them with the longest-stemmed flowers, scabious perhaps, and continue with the next longest and so on until the leaves are covered with a graduated fan shape of garden blooms. Tie the stems with a wide satin ribbon or, country style, with plaited raffia.

LONG-LASTING
PRESENTATION POSY

*Choose the toughest, most long-lasting flowers
when you're making up a posy to present to a
visitor – perhaps a guest speaker. Two-tone Doris
pinks, white spray carnations, and pink and white
daisy chrysanthemums are practical and pretty too.
Arrange alternate rings of pinks and carnations,
surrounding them first with the daisy-shaped
flowers and then with gypsophila. Add a protective
collar of glossy magnolia leaves; bind the stems
with fine wire and then – for a comfortable grip –
with ribbon. Present the posy with pride!*

A Trio of
Miniature Posies

*Children can fashion the smallest floral snippings
into perfect posies. A handful of love-in-a-mist
(nigella), candytuft, daisies, pinks, pansies, and
gypsophila — that's the stuff that miniature posies
are made of. Fold 3 paper doilies into 4, snip off
the corner of each and push a posy through the
hole. Secure with sticky or Scotch tape around the
stems, and display each posy in a spice jar or tiny
glass. A trio makes a pretty table centrepiece.*

37

A Posy of Victorian Foliage

*Select a handful of leaves in the brightest colours
you can find to make a table centrepiece posy in
the Victorian tradition. Arrange the foliage in a
circle on a large flat plate, stems toward the
centre, in overlapping rings. You could, for
example, have an outer ring of maple, followed by
a ring of lime, then geranium (the frilled kinds are
prettiest), then yellow-spotted laurel, and purple
and green variegated ivy. One perfect flower hides
the stems in the centre: what could be daintier than
a fully-opened yellow rose?*

BUTTERCUPS
& DAISIES

*Capture the joy of a child's first impromptu
buttercups and daisies posy and create one, slightly
more formal, with larger blooms. Take a bunch of
buttercup-yellow ranunculus and daisy-shaped
marguerites and shape them into a full, round
posy. Edge the ring of flowers with trailing ivy,
and tie the stems with long, supple grasses.*

41

THE JOY OF AN OLD-FASHIONED ROSE

Flatter a fully opened and sweetly scented old-fashioned rose – it might be a magenta-pink centifolia (cabbage) rose or a purple moss rose – by encircling it with aromatic leaves. Gather a handful of downy sage, spiky lavender and decorative sweet cecily, carrot or dill foliage, and arrange them around the rose stem. Bind the stems together and place the posy in a small sparkling glass carafe or scent bottle.

43

A Gift for Mother's Day

*A perfect mother's day gift. You will need a bunch
of freesias, a few yellow and white ranunculus, a
bunch of anemones and some trails of ivy. Arrange
the freesias in a cluster, ring the tight ranunculus
flowerheads around them, and encircle the posy
with anemones. Add a few trails of ivy and bind
the stems. Display the posy in a pretty hankie:
place the stem ends toward the centre, gather up
the sides, and tie it just beneath the flowerheads.*

45

CHRISTMAS MISTLETOE CLUSTER

Take a handful of mistletoe, a few sprays of ivy, and some red rosebuds, fresh or dried. Place long stems of ivy flat on a table, arrange the rosebuds in a fan shape on top, and fill in the spaces with white-berried mistletoe. Tie the stems with red ribbon and hang the posy, romantically, over a headboard. A miniature version of the posy makes a delightful gift trimming.

JEWEL-COLOURED VICTORIAN POSY

Make a posy in all the rich blues, purples, and reds that were popular in Victorian times. It would make a charming gift for an aunt or an older friend. Gather an armful of long-stemmed sapphire blue sage and anchusa (bugloss or borage) flowers, deep amethyst marjoram and chive flowers, and ruby-red antirrhinum and sweet William, and compose them into a sheaf, longest stems at the back, shortest ones at the front. Tie the posy with a deep, deep blue ribbon.

49

ROMANTIC BEDROOM BOUQUET

*Gather the prettiest dried flowers you can find, and
tie them into a dainty posy to hang on a bedpost
or a bedroom chair. There may be 2 or 3 pink and
cream rosebuds, a handful of lime-green lady's
mantle and creamy-white sea lavender, and a
couple of stems of pink larkspur. Compose them in
your hand to make a fan-shaped posy – the
longest stems at the back, the shortest at the front.
Bind and then hang the posy with
pure white ribbons.*

A Posy of Dried Flowers

Take a few stems of dried broom in yellow, pink, and crimson, some dried pink and white helipterum (rhodanthe), a handful of dried gypsophila, and some dried coral-coloured rosebuds. On a table top, arrange the broom to make a graceful fan shape. Cover it with the daisy-shaped helipterum, and a generous bunch of gypsophila. Push in the rosebuds to complete the posy. Tie the stems with ribbons and place the posy on a shelf or a dresser.

53

A GARDEN OF
EVERGREEN FOLIAGE

*The Victorians loved blending foliage in richly
contrasting textures and colours and then, for a
more striking effect, adding nuts and fruit. Copy
the idea for a winter centrepiece. Take a handful of
almonds, pecans and kumquats, and twist them
onto medium-thick wires. Make a posy of spiky
juniper, glossy bay, and downy sage leaves.
Arrange the nuts and fruits to form circles among
the leaves. Bind the stems together and place the
posy in a glistening glass container.*

EASTERTIME
EGGSHELL POSIES

—

*Break 3 or 4 eggs near the top, tip out the contents
and wash the shells. Use these pretty little vases
for a group of Easter posies. Choose tiny flowers
like forget-me-not, pulmonaria ("lords and
ladies"), primulas and heart's-ease. Make them
into tiny bunches, and arrange them to trail over
the sides of the containers. A single eggshell posy
makes a dainty decoration for an Easter cake.*

Thank You Posy

When you want to give a posy to express your thanks, use the Victorian floral language to "say it with flowers". Take blue campanula and white bellflower, which both signify gratitude, and daffodils for "kind regards". Compose them into a free-style posy, letting the softly-flowing lines of the stems determine the shape. Ring the posy with fern leaves for "sincerity" and sweet basil for "best wishes".

A POSY TO TOP A PAGEBOY'S STAFF

When small pageboys carry flowers, the posy looks
best attached to a bamboo staff. Cut a piece of
bamboo about a foot long and paint it white. Wire
onto one end 3 long, narrow mauve liatris (Kansas
gayfeather) flowers and surround them with a
circle of short-stemmed bunches of gypsophila.
Wire 6 or 7 peach-coloured daisy chrysanthemums
around the outside, and surround them with
variegated ivy leaves. Bind the stems with narrow
ribbon and leave trailing ends.

CHRISTMAS
WELCOME POSY

Hang an evergreen posy on your door and highlight it with a touch of pure Victoriana – a tartan bow. Take 2 or 3 knobbly twigs – apple wood is ideal – and some long stems of laurel, holly, ivy, cypress, whatever you have. Arrange the twigs and evergreens flat on a table in a fan shape, then twist wire around some tiny apples, nuts, and cones, and attach. Bind the stems with wire and add a hook for hanging. Be generous with the tartan ribbon for the bow.

63

Pamela Westland has written extensively on the art of flower arranging; her works include *A Creative Guide to Flowering Arranging* and *Flowers with Style,* as well as many magazine articles. She also appears on television.

Gill Tomblin studied art at the Bath Academy and the Central School in London. She has always been interested in botany and natural history, and is a founder member of The Society of Botanical Artists. As well as regularly exhibiting in galleries, she has illustrated a number of books, including *New Formal Gardens*, by Sir Roy Strong, *Town Gardens*, and *Creative Gardening* for Reader's Digest.